Where Is My Daddy?

By Geoff Jackson

2

I don't understand why
My dad's gone away,
We laughed and we giggled
And played every day.

It's nothing you've said and

You've done nothing wrong,

He loved you so dearly,

With you he belonged.

His body was weak, much

Too weak to survive,

He died, it's so sad, he's

No longer alive.

Just like mobile phone your

dad's power got low,

It would not recharge and

Was his time to go.

But what is important,

The one thing that's true,

Your dad was so happy,

Because he had you.

Each moment spent with you,

It brightened his day,

He thought you were perfect,

In every good way.

So where is my daddy?

Does anyone know?

A garden in Heaven's

Where he had to go.

A place where he's happy,

It's where he must stay,

He'll check on you often,

Almost every day.

Although you can't see him,

He's always close by,

So tell him you love him,

And say reasons why.

I'm all ears, talk to me

He hears what you're saying,

And smiling at you,

He sends hugs and kisses,

And misses you too.

I love you and I hear you

So when you are lonely,

And missing your dad,

Remember him laughing,

And good times you had.

Sometimes you'll feel sad and

It's ok to cry,

You'll need hugs and cuddles

From people close by.

It may also help if

You talk and you share,

The great times with daddy,

And how life's not fair.

The days will get better,

The pain will soon fade,

Remember with fondness,

The memories you made.

For daddy was special,

His best friend was you,

You made him so happy,

He'll always love you.

Printed in Great Britain
by Amazon

36913425R00021